BY PAT GOFFE AND LOIS HOWARD

Trust & Obey

A WHALE'S TALE

"The story of Jonah"

Paper Back Cover ISBN Number: 13:978-0-9970612-5-3

Library of Congress Number: 2019901128

Published By Pat Goffe/Pat Goffe Publishing

To inquire about booking Pat Goffe or Lois Howard for a speaking engagement, book signing or a reading, please contact:

Pat Goffe's Contact
Email: pat@patgoffeauthor.com
Website: www.patgoffeauthor.com
Contact Number: (904) 520-1898

Lois Howard's Contact
Email: howardmar7771@gmail.com
Contact Number: (772)-333-0442

It was one of those days you dream of. The ocean was calm. The sun was bright and shiny, beckoning me to experience its warmth and embrace.

I dove deep, did a complete turn, and began swimming as fast as I could toward the surface.

I couldn't wait! I exploded through the surface of the water and leaped high into the air. I felt the kiss of the sun and the hug of my Creator. What a day! The Creator was using me.

Let me tell you why I was so excited. I was minding my own business, hunting and feasting on my afternoon snacks in the ocean. As a whale, I need a lot of food to survive. I was having all my favorites: fish, shrimp, larvae, plankton, crabs, krill, and squid. For some reason I was eating much more than usual, as if food were going out of style!

I was using echolocation. That means sending out a vibration and listening for the sound waves to reflect back to determine whether there was prey, predator or an inanimate object in front of me. I continued to create these vibrations until I heard something.

The sound was unfamiliar and it startled me. Instead of swimming away I continued to listen, waiting. I then realized it wasn't my next meal. It was my Creator!

I couldn't believe it. The Creator was talking to me. WOW. Growing up, my grandmother always talked about the Creator, God. She taught us about Him and how He created sea creatures on the fifth day. As He talked to me I made sure to listen to Him very carefully, as I would when hunting for my prey. I didn't want to make any mistakes.

God wanted me to go on a special mission for Him. The Creator instructed me to head toward Tarshish. He told me I would run into a huge storm, and there I would find a man named Jonah who would be thrown off a big ship.

A huge storm? I was taught by my grandmother to always swim away from storms.

The Creator continued to talk to me. I was to swallow Jonah whole, but I wasn't allowed to snack on him. Good thing I'd already eaten. I didn't understand how all of this was supposed to play out, but one thing I did know was OBEDIENCE! My grandmother taught me to always obey the Creator.

I was afraid of the storm that God was going to start and what would happen to Jonah. But the Creator comforted and reassured me that He would protect me. "We are not to run *from* God, *but to* Him. As Proverbs 18:10 says, "The name of the Lord is a strong tower; the righteous man runs into it and is safe."

PROVERBS 18:10
"THE NAME OF THE LORD IS
A STRONG TOWER THE
RIGHTEOUS MAN
RUNS INTO IT AND
IS SAFE"

12

I swam and swam as fast as I could, so I could be where the Creator instructed me to be. If I arrived a moment too late this ending would be a sad moment for Jonah.

I heard my best friend say, "Come and play hide and seek with us."

I stopped for a moment to say, "I can't today." I was determined to stay focused. God was counting on me.

14

As I swam in Jonah's direction at times the waves were very rough and pushing me off course. The loud, continuous roar of thunder was a sure indication that I was approaching the destination the Creator had instructed me to find.

I could've chosen to give up, but I was determined to be obedient. I looked around and there it was the big ship in a terrible storm. I saw the humans lift Jonah high in the air, ready to fling him overboard. I positioned myself to make sure I was ready to take Jonah in.

As soon as they flung Jonah overboard, the sea stopped raging, the waves became calm, and the thunder and lightning ceased in the blink of an eye. Just as God started the storm, He stopped it. The Creator is AMAZING. Even the winds and the waves obey Him.

The men on the ship also marveled at my Creator's majestic power. My keen hearing allowed me to hear the men on the ship praying to the Lord promising to always obey Him. What an awesome testimony.

I dove and swam as quickly as I could to find Jonah. There he was at the bottom of the sea tangled up with seaweed wrapped around his head. I opened my mouth wide and scooped him up.

Poor Jonah. I had no idea what he had done. I knew he had to be very uncomfortable in my dark, cold, stinky belly filled with fish, shrimp, larvae, plankton, crabs, krill, and squid.

Jonah sat in my belly for a while. I heard him cry out loud as he called out to the Lord. He was begging and pleading for God's forgiveness. "Lord, I'm sorry for being disobedient and not going to Nineveh as you instructed. I knew you were trying to get my attention when that huge storm came. When the captain of the ship woke me up, he asked me, "Why aren't you praying to your God? How are you able to sleep through this terrible storm so peacefully?"

"Lord, I had to confess and let them know I was the cause of the raging storm. I told the captain, 'Throw me overboard. As soon as you throw me overboard, my God will stop the raging storm. Now here I am, in the belly of this whale. Lord, I promise I will be obedient to your will and to your ways. I will share your good news with the people of Nineveh. I will let them know that you are the one and only true God, and how much you love them, in spite of their wicked ways. Please just spare my life.'

I was shocked to hear what Jonah was saying. I had no idea until now why I had to go and get Jonah. Did he really think he could hide from the Creator? Those crazy humans, I thought my friends and I were silly for playing hide and seek, as big as we are. Don't they know you can't hide from God? He is omnipresent . . . because He is everywhere.

I'm reminded of Jeremiah 23:24 that says, "'Can a man hide himself in secret places so that I cannot see him?' declares the LORD. 'Do I not fill heaven and earth?' declares the LORD."

How dare he think it was okay to disobey the Creator. Not for a minute would I try to second guess the Creator or even consider disobeying Him. I had to catch myself as those thoughts ran through my mind. I realized in the midst of my thoughts it wasn't for me to judge or be hard on Jonah just as Jonah shouldn't judge the evil people of Nineveh. I immediately whispered a prayer asking my Creator to forgive me for judging Jonah.

CREATOR,
FORGIVE ME

While I was talking to the Creator, I felt a terrible pain. I became dizzy and my stomach started to rumble as if it were under attack. That's when it hit me. I hadn't had a meal in three days.

It was then I heard the Creator say, "I will deliver you from this agonizing pain. It is now time for you to deliver Jonah." Without hesitation I swam towards the shore and spewed Jonah out.

I sure wish humans would learn to obey the Creator like those of us created on the fifth day. Oh well, maybe one day, I thought, as I happily swam away